D0099580

BASKETBALL

FROM TIP-OFF TO SLAM DUNK—THE ESSENTIAL GUIDE

Copyright © Kingfisher 2012
Published in the United States by Kingfisher,
175 Fifth Ave., New York, NY 10010
Kingfisher is an imprint of Macmillan Children's Books, London.
All rights reserved.

Distributed in the U.S. and Canada by Macmillan, 175 Fifth Ave., New York, NY 10010

Library of Congress Cataloging-in-Publication data has been applied for.

ISBN: 978-0-7534-6872-2

Kingfisher books are available for special promotions and premiums. For details contact: Special Markets Department, Macmillan, 175 Fifth Ave., New York, NY 10010.

For more information, please visit www.kingfisherbooks.com

Printed in China
1 3 5 7 9 8 6 4 2
1TR/0412/WKT/UTD/140MA

Photography by Michael Wicks

With thanks to Northamptonshire Basketball Club, U.K. and John Collins, Karen Goodrich, Katie Bayliss, Sarah Round, Caitlin Stewart, Amy Boot, Steph Ogden, Jami Luu, Tara Hings, Jacob Round, Ollie Thomas, Luke Joines, Josh Round, Andre Arissol, Declan Burke, Pauli Laurinolli, and Carlo Nieva

BASKETBALL

FROM TIP-OFF TO SLAM DUNK—THE ESSENTIAL GUIDE

CLIVE GIFFORD

KINGFISHER
NEW YORK

Contents

Hoop dreams

Fast, furious, and enormous fun for players and spectators, basketball is an action-packed team sport. Two teams pass, dribble, and shoot the ball, hoping to score baskets worth one, two, or three points. Games are usually high scoring, with 150–220 points typically scored during a professional game.

Basketball began when a group of students needed to be kept entertained in a gym during the winter. James Naismith devised the sport while teaching at a college in Springfield, Massachusetts, in 1891. He drew up a list of 13 rules, which have been added to greatly. In the United States, teams often follow rules set by the NCAA and the NBA. In the rest of the world, the game's international governing body, called FIBA, sets slightly different rules, which are followed at the Olympics.

Two players challenge for a ball under a basket. Defensive players will try to block passes, deny the other team open space, and steal possession.

Dr. James Naismith, the inventor of basketball, holds a ball and a wooden peach basket that acted as the first hoop and net in basketball.

"Even when I'm old and gray, I won't be able to play it, but I'll still love the game."

Michael Jordan, NBA legend

For every pro basketball player, there are tens of thousands of enthusiastic amateurs around the world. They regularly enjoy a casual game of basketball, like these students and trainee monks in Qinghai, China.

Australian and Canadian wheelchair athletes battle under the basket during the gold medal match at the 2008 Paralympic Games.

As well as the regular five-on-five basketball game, there are several variations, including street ball and beach basketball. Developed during the 1940s, wheelchair basketball has now become one of the most popular sports at the Paralympic Games.

A young Romanian fan is dazzled by the ball handling skills of a player from the Harlem Globetrotters. Formed as an African-American team in 1926, the Globetrotters have used their own brand of tricks and skills to entertain millions of fans.

Joe Johnson of the Atlanta Hawks scores during a 2011 NBA game against the Chicago Bulls. The National Basketball Association (NBA) is made up of 30 teams featuring the world's best players.

PARALYMPIC GAMES: a multisport event held shortly after the Olympics for elite athletes with disabilities

Basketball terms

A numbers game

Many of basketball's rules are all about numbers—from the 15-minute intermission in the middle of the game to the number of personal fouls allowed. Most fundamental of all is a game's duration, which for NBA games is four quarters of 12 minutes, while NCAA games have two halves of 20 minutes. FIBA games have four quarters of 10 minutes. If the score is tied at the end, then a short period of overtime is usually played.

Despite being under pressure from an opponent, the offensive player has put up a shot in open play. If the shot is successful, his team will score two points and play begins from the scoring team's end line.

For a basket to be scored, the ball must complete its journey down and through the hoop. Shots from close to the hoop score two points, while shots outside of the three-point line score three points. Free throws score one point each.

A coach indicates to the game officials that he wants to take a time-out. The officials stop the game and the clock.

Seconds count in basketball . . . A team must bring the ball past the midcourt line within eight seconds of receiving it, or a backcourt violation occurs and the opposing team is given the ball. When making a throw-in from the sideline, a player has just five seconds to pass the ball in bounds; otherwise possession goes to the other team.

The shot clock shows the time limit within which a team with the ball must shoot. In NBA and FIBA games, this time limit is 24 seconds, but it is often a little longer in games for younger players. A team is also allowed a number of time-outs. These breaks in play are usually one minute long and give teams a chance to regroup and listen to their coach's instructions.

With two seconds on the shot clock remaining, Javier Gonzalez nails a three-point shot for his NCAA team, North Carolina State University, during a 2010 game against Duke University.

Three-point line

Marked at each end of a basketball court is a large arc—the three-point line. A successful shot made from outside of this line will net the shooter's team three points.

Free-throw line

Player taking a free throw

Players must stand around edge of the free-throw line

A foul by one team during a game may result in one or more free throws. These are taken from the free-throw line directly in front of the basket and are worth one point each. A player has ten seconds to take a free throw; otherwise, the attempt is lost.

Although a team has five players on the court during a game, these five can swap with other players on the team, called substitutes or reserves. Smart use of substitutions by a team's coach can be the difference between winning and losing.

> *"Everything negative— pressure, challenges— is an opportunity for me to rise."*
>
> *Kobe Bryant, NBA star*

On the court

The basketball court is where all of your basketball triumphs and defeats will take place. Get used to your local court's lighting and the out-of-bounds areas surrounding the court—you're going to spend a lot of time here. Indoor courts are usually made from sprung wooden floors, while outdoor courts may be covered with concrete or an all-weather surface. At each end stands a post holding a backboard and basket.

A tip-off is used to start the game from the middle of the center circle. The official throws the ball into the air and players try to out-jump their opponent to tip the ball to a teammate.

Backboard marked with inner square 24 in. (60cm) by 18 in. (45cm) in size

6 in. (15cm) distance between backboard and back of rim

The hoop is 18 in. (46cm) in diameter

Post holds hoop 10 ft. (3.05m) above the court

The basket consists of the hoop with a net attached. This is attached to a large board called the backboard, from which the ball can rebound into the hoop or back into play.

The courts used for NBA and U.S. college basketball games are 94 ft. (28.65m) long and 50 ft. (15.24m) wide. The courts used for U.S. high school basketball games are usually 10 ft. (3.05m) shorter. FIBA basketball courts are 91.8 ft. (28m) by 49.2 ft. (15m). In all adult versions of the sport, the basket is at the same height—10 ft. (3.05m) above the floor.

Sidelines and end lines mark the boundaries of the court—if the ball crosses one of these lines, it is out of play. The midcourt line (division line) separates the court into two halves. Your backcourt contains the basket that you are defending, and your frontcourt contains the basket into which you shoot.

Free-throw lane (also called the lane) or the paint

Hoop attached to backboard

Free-throw line

NBA court

Three-point line

Sideline

End line

Midcourt line

Center circle

The boundary lines of the court (sidelines and end lines) are not part of the playing area. So if you are standing on a boundary line while in contact with the ball, then the ball is out of bounds.

When the ball goes out of play over one of the boundary lines, the game is restarted with a throw-in. The team that did not touch the ball last gets possession.

Once your team has taken the ball over the midcourt line, there's no turning back. If you dribble or pass back into your backcourt, the official will signal a violation and the ball will be handed to the opposing team.

Offensive players can stay in the lane for only three seconds. They will usually move in and out of this restricted area looking for a pass or rebound opportunity. If they spend longer than three seconds in the lane, the referee signals a three-second violation.

Basketball terms **VIOLATION:** a breaking of a rule of the game that usually results in the ball passing to the other team

Prepare to play

Preparation is key to success in a game. It involves warming up well so that your muscles are ready for the intense effort ahead. It also means checking that your uniform is in good order and you are fully focused on the challenges ahead. You may be playing in a new, unfamiliar position or finding yourself up against a highly talented opponent, so you will need to be at your very best from the start.

Three players perform a move called a Russian march to stretch their leg muscles. Stretching muscles before playing improves performance and can reduce the chances of injury.

Jersey tucked into shorts ————

A player's basketball uniform includes a loose-fitting jersey that does not restrict their movement, a pair of shorts, and often team socks and shoes. Some players also like to wear sweatbands on their wrists to wipe away sweat during a game. Your socks should be able to absorb moisture from your feet and provide some cushioning.

PRO TIPS
Take your preparation seriously and commit fully to each warm-up exercise and drill. Lazy players who don't prepare well rarely perform at their best.

Sport socks

With all the sharp turning, jumping, and sprinting, basketball can be very hard on your feet. As a result, you need a good pair of basketball shoes. These help support your ankles, cushion your feet, and give you good grip on the court floor.

Warm-up drills

These players are performing warm-up drills before a game. Such drills may involve shooting from different parts of the court, dribble relays, and ball-handling drills that emphasize quick passing and movement. They are all designed to prepare you for the game.

At a young age, you are likely to play all over the court. As you get older, however, your coach may ask you to specialize in a certain position. Although positions can be flexible and tactics vary, there are five commonly used playing positions with which many teams start a game.

Shooting guard—usually a team's best shooter, as they are likely to attempt plenty of longer-distance shots during a game. When defending, the shooting guard usually defends against the opposing team's best guard.

Point guard—usually the fastest player on the team. The point guard must organize the team's offense, controlling the ball and timing initial passes and moves.

Hair pulled back, if long

Make sure all jewelry is removed

Power forward—big and strong, the power forward can expect to play close to the basket, as they look for passes, short drives, turn-and-jump shots, and rebounds.

Small forward—rarely small on professional teams, but an explosive player who is expected to dribble, drive, and cut toward the basket.

Make sure shoelaces are tied firmly and that all straps are fastened securely

Center—along with the power forward, usually the tallest player on the court. The center tries to score from close to the basket and must stay alert for rebounds.

REBOUNDING: the skill of regaining the ball after a failed shot has bounced off the hoop or backboard

Basketball terms

Receiving the ball

Receiving the ball well calls for good technique, confidence, and focus. A poor catch can lead to dropping the ball, giving the opposing team a chance to gain possession and score. Good catching technique involves keeping your arms relaxed and your hands soft so that they move back as the ball arrives. Stiff hands often result in the ball bouncing out of a player's grasp.

Head up, with eyes scanning the court ahead

Fingers of both hands spread around the ball

Spotting an incoming pass, this player has his hands up and out in front. With the ball coming in at above waist height, his thumbs are inside and his palms are facing the ball.

The player has moved toward the ball, watching it fall right into his hands. His arms and hands pull back to draw the ball into his body.

With the ball caught, get into the triple-threat stance. This sees you stand with a wide base, knees flexed, head up, and the ball in front of your chest. With your body balanced, you can move in any direction to make a dribble, shot, or pass. Guarding against all three threats is very difficult, which is why getting into this position quickly is so important.

Weight on the balls of the feet

The player has his feet a little wider than shoulder width apart, and his head is up. This is called the triple-threat stance because there are three things he can now do—shoot, pass, or dribble.

When the ball is coming in low, try to catch it with your little fingers on the inside and with your palms facing upward.

Try to catch a high pass with both of your hands. If you cannot get both hands to the ball, try to use one hand to bat the ball back toward you and then catch it.

To catch a high ball, time your jump and stretch your arms up quickly. Try to catch the ball in front of you so you can watch it go right into your hands.

Passes from teammates are rarely perfect in the heat of a game. Keep your eye on the ball, your body ready to react, and your hands soft. This will allow you to gather in many poorly made or deflected passes that arrive higher, lower, or more to the side than you would like.

Masterclass

Kevin Durant

Having received the ball expertly, Kevin Durant of the Oklahoma City Thunder swivels his upper body away to protect it. Good hands, vision, and superb shooting have seen Durant lead the NBA points scoring table for two seasons. He was also voted MVP at the 2010 FIBA World Championships.

These young players are practicing their receiving skills by fielding short passes from their coach. These passes are made at a variety of heights, speeds, and angles.

Passing

Passing is the most common skill you will use in a game, so it pays to practice it as often as you can. Passing involves more than just perfecting each of the different pass techniques. It also involves learning when and where to use each type of pass, where to target your pass, and gauging how much force to use.

Get both hands on the ball, with your fingers spread around the sides and back of the ball. This will give you a good grip.

This player has received the ball at just above waist height. She spots a teammate in an open space who can receive a pass. She brings the ball up in front of the center of her chest and close to her body.

1

One foot must stay in contact with the floor

Taking a step toward the receiver, the passer straightens her elbows to push the ball forward. She leans into the pass but keeps her head level and her eyes on the target. A short, quick chest pass can be made without the step.

2

Passing moves the ball around the court faster than a player can dribble it. The chest pass is one of the quickest passes to make because the ball is played from in front of your chest—close to the triple-threat stance.

"It doesn't matter who scores the points; it's who can get the ball to the scorer."

Larry Bird, Boston Celtics legend

PRO TIPS

Practice chest passes with your receiver on the move. Aim the right distance in front of them so that they do not have to break their stride.

To make an overhead pass, raise the ball up above your head with both hands.

With your feet shoulder width apart, snap your wrists forward to release the ball.

Keep your arms moving so they end with your forearms parallel to the court floor.

As the arms straighten, the passer snaps her wrists so that the backs of both hands face each other with the fingers pointing to the target. The ball should fly on a flat path and arrive at the receiver at around chest height.

The overhead pass is an underrated pass—it works especially well when you fake to dribble or pass low and then reach up to make the pass. In youth basketball, where players may vary greatly in height, it is a good pass to make over the outstretched arms of a defender who is much shorter than you.

Your coach may suggest a wide range of different drills and games for you to practice your passing. Here, four players stride down the court, exchanging chest passes as quickly and as accurately as possible.

Basketball terms | **FAKE:** to pretend to make a play or a move in one direction in order to unbalance an opponent

More passing

Bounce passes and baseball passes are other types of passes you should try to perfect in training and practice. A greater variety of passes will help with a wide range of game situations. A short bounce pass will keep the ball in your team's possession, while a fast break opportunity may need a long baseball pass from deep in your backcourt.

Fingers around back and sides of the ball

Bending low at the knees, the player steps to her right with her left foot so that she keeps her body between the ball and her opponent.

This player spots a teammate who is open and decides to make a bounce pass with her right hand under the arms of an opponent.

A bounce pass is a pass made from around waist height, with the ball driven into the court floor so it bounces up to be caught by your receiver at waist height. Bounce passes can be made with one or two hands. The one-handed version is often used at the end of a dribble. Bounce passes can be used all over the court but especially when an opponent is close by and has their arms up, such as after you have faked a shot.

This player is making a bounce pass with his left hand. He has stepped forward using his right foot so that his body shields the ball from his opponent.

Learning which pass to use in a particular situation comes only with lots of experience. Try to build your passing skills in practice and also off the court with one or more friends. Aim to perfect your passes from both sides of your body to maximize your passing threat.

The passer aims to bounce the ball about two-thirds of the distance between herself and the receiver. Once the pass is made, she will move into open space away from her defender as quickly as possible.

3

To make a long-distance, two-handed baseball pass up the court, take the ball back to one side of your head.

Like a throw in baseball, the ball is thrust forward with the arms extending and is then released with a quick snap of the wrist.

Two players practice their passes during a team practice session. One player performs a chest pass, while the other player performs a bounce pass at the same time.

Basketball terms **OPEN:** used to describe a player on the offensive team who is in a position to receive a pass

Basic dribbling

Dribbling can move the ball up the court, get you into a better position, or be used as you make a powerful drive to the basket. It should be a smooth, controlled movement, with one hand on the top half of the ball and only the pads of your fingers making contact. Never slap the ball with your hand.

A low dribble sees the player bend his knees and extend his dribbling arm downward, keeping the ball moving smoothly on its short journey up and down.

Keep the amount of force consistent to help you build rhythm. Control and direction are crucial. Many beginners make the mistake of driving the ball too close to their feet and overrunning the ball, or directing the ball too far ahead of themselves. As a result, they will either lose control or have the ball stolen from them by an opponent.

The player keeps his knees flexed and his body slightly forward. His head is up and level. The elbow of his dribbling hand is kept close to his body, and the ball is controlled with his fingertips spread out over the top of the ball.

Head up, with eyes scanning the court for threats and opportunities

As he moves forward, the player drives the ball down and a little ahead of himself with a flexing of his wrist.

Arm extends with fingers pointing down

1

2

Dribbling carries the risk of a steal, so always dribble with a purpose and stay aware of threats from all directions. Whenever possible, protect the ball by putting your body between the ball and an opponent. You can pivot and switch dribbling hands. However, if both hands touch the ball simultaneously and you continue dribbling, you will have committed a violation and your opponents will receive the ball.

This player tries to drive past a player from the other team, keeping the ball on the side of her body farthest away from her opponent.

PRO TIPS

Top players work tirelessly in practice so that they can dribble well with either hand. This allows them to get past opponents on either side.

Letting your dribbling hand slip under the ball results in a carrying, or palming, violation. Possession passes to the other team.

With his elbow remaining close to his body, the player lets his wrist bend upward to help cushion the ball's rise before driving it back down to the floor again.

The player repeats the process. A good dribble up the court sees the player pump the ball with rhythm so that it bounces up under control.

Wrist flexes upward to receive the ball before driving it down again

3

4

Finding space

A basketball court can seem like a small, crowded place, especially when the action occurs in and around the lanes. Even so, there are always open spaces you can move into to help your team keep possession and advance your team's offensive play. The key is to stay alert and with your head up, looking for opportunities.

As soon as you have made an accurate pass, try to move away swiftly and positively into a good space to receive the ball. You may receive an immediate return pass, so stay alert.

You will often find yourself guarded on the court by an opponent who moves as you do. Their aim is to deny you space and time to receive the ball and make a scoring play. Getting away from your defender is a priority. A sudden change of pace or a move in another direction can sometimes get you free, especially if they are timed so that a teammate can pass to you as you get free.

Playing three-on-three is an excellent way to work on your movement and your communication with teammates and to learn where good pockets of space can be found on court.

Offensive player's movement must be convincing

Drives hard off the balls of his feet

Faking a movement in one direction can help you get free of an opponent and into an open space. The offensive player in blue has stepped to his left, looking as if he is about to receive a pass out wide in that direction.

The defender moves to his right to cover his opponent's movement, but as he does so, the offensive player drives hard off his left foot to change direction, cutting sharply to his right.

Masterclass

Cappie Poindexter

U.S. national team and WNBA star Cappie Poindexter fires off a one-handed pass after cutting free of her defender. Highly mobile, Poindexter has won two WNBA championships with the Phoenix Mercury as well as a 2008 Olympic gold medal.

Teammates can work together to make an open space for one of them to move into. Moves include doubling back to create space ahead of you and setting a screen (see pp. 44–45). Another move is to cut sharply to the side to look like you are expecting to receive the ball. This may draw an opponent, creating a space for your teammate to drive into.

The player in blue (on the right) is performing a backdoor cut. He has moved away from the basket, drawing his defender, before cutting back sharply behind the defender and toward the basket to receive a well-timed pass.

Offensive player's arm up, asking for ball

3

If you get free from your defender, make sure you are in a good position to receive a pass.

4

As he sprints away, the offensive player signals for the ball. The defender has overcommitted to his right and cannot get back into position quickly enough to prevent a completed pass.

This defender is not chasing back and will be out of the game for several passes. If your defender reacts quickly, try to make another cut or fake just as they are getting back into position.

Pivoting and fakes

You may often receive the ball facing the wrong way or with an opponent in the way of your next move. Fortunately, there are a number of techniques you can perform easily to help you get into position or make the move you want. With all of these pivoting and fake moves, ensure you keep your balance, with your knees flexed a little.

Hands up to receive ball

Body weight over the left foot, which acts as the pivot foot

Right foot steps around

Player swivels on ball of left foot

Feet aligned as player shoots

This player receives the ball with her back to the basket. She establishes her left foot as her pivot foot and then steps around to face the basket.

As you receive the ball, you can establish a pivot foot. This foot cannot be moved, but it can be swiveled or rotated on the spot as you step around with your other foot. Pivoting in this way allows you to face the direction you want. If you take a step with your pivot foot, you will be guilty of traveling.

This player fakes to pass low and to his left. As the defender leans or steps over to try to block the pass, the player whips the ball back in front and releases a shot before the defender can recover.

Offensive player's eyes face direction of fake pass

Defender steps and leans to cover pass

Offensive player moves ball back in front of body

PRO TIPS

"Selling" the fake to your opponent is key to its success. Make your fake look as realistic as possible and fix your eyes on the basket if faking a shot.

Defender's arms rise upward to block possible shot

Offensive player brings arms down sharply

With defender unbalanced, offensive player makes a chest pass to the side

Offensive player eyes basket as she fakes a shot

Facing the basket, this offensive player moves the ball from low to high as if she is about to perform a jump shot. She keeps the balls of her feet on the ground. As the defender rises or even jumps, space appears to the side, allowing the offensive player to make a pass without the risk of it being blocked.

Jump shot released

Fakes and feints are simply pretending to do one thing to unbalance an opponent before doing something else. When handling the ball, you can fake a pass before actually shooting or you can fake a pass in one direction, making the defender commit themselves, and then pass in another direction.

The no-look pass can be a great way to throw off an opponent. However, it should be performed only over short distances, and you should be absolutely certain that a teammate is there.

Masterclass

Steve Nash

The Phoenix Suns' Steve Nash dribbles into the lane after making a fake to help him drive forward. Nash's quick hands and reactions have made him one of the great playmakers in the NBA. A fine passer of the ball, he has averaged the most assists per game in five different NBA seasons.

Shooting

All players can contribute to a team with accurate shooting to score points. The set shot is made with feet on the ground and chest square to the target. Many players use it to make free throws. Jump shots are used all over the court, both for three-pointers and for short-range shots where a leap upward and good arm extension can send the ball up and over a defender's outstretched arms.

Accurate shooting starts with body alignment and balance. For most types of shots, you must face the basket, with your eyes fixed on the rim. The foot on the side of your shooting hand should be slightly ahead of the other to give a stable base. Young players sometimes struggle with shooting longer distances. Remember that with all set and jump shots, much of the thrust of the shot comes from your legs bending, and then straightening. A good, firm leg drive means you won't force the ball away, which tends to lead to a snatched shot.

Your hands and fingers should follow through after a shot. Think of your hand reaching down into a cookie jar.

Eyes should focus on the basket rim

Shooting hand underneath the ball

Legs straightened

PRO TIPS

You can create more space for a shot by stepping forward with your nonpivot foot, forcing the defender back, before stepping back and making a shot.

1 To make a set shot, start with your feet shoulder width apart, with your shoulders and toes pointing toward the basket.

2 As you straighten your legs and rise, extend your arms. The elbow of your shooting arm should be under the ball.

3 Release your supporting hand, push the ball away with your arm, and release the ball with a snap of your wrist and fingers.

Masterclass

Dirk Nowitzki

Dirk Nowitzki shows great technique when taking a jump shot. His elbow is directly under the ball, and his head is level and still. The German forward has spent all of his NBA career with the Dallas Mavericks, where his shooting accuracy includes making 88 percent of his free throws.

Work on your shooting whenever you can. Take each shot seriously and analyze what is going wrong if many miss the target. Shots repeatedly heading wide on one side show that you are not aligning yourself properly to the basket. Get your coach to watch you carefully and suggest what is wrong. Small adjustments can often mean great improvements.

Ball travels on a high path up and then down into the basket

Fingers follow through to end up pointing toward the floor

Keep your elbow under the ball right up to the point when you release the shot.

1

To make a jump shot, crouch low with your back straight but your knees bent, and with your head and body square to the target.

2

Spring straight up from the balls of both feet, keeping your back straight and the elbow of your shooting arm under the ball.

3

Extend and straighten your arms as you rise, and release the ball with a strong flick of your wrists and fingers.

Lay-ups and drives

A lay-up is a one-handed shot made after a driving play to the basket. It relies on a springy bound to get close to the basket, followed by a powerful leap up to get your shooting hand as close to the hoop as possible. The ball is released gently to bounce off the backboard and down through the basket.

Try to release the ball with your fingers at the very highest point of your jump.

Palm of hand faces the backboard

When under no defensive pressure—if you are open on a fast break, for example—lay-ups can be an easy way to score, as long as you keep good rhythm, time your step, and jump to the basket correctly. Gauge your distance accurately— once you place the ball in both hands, each foot can touch the floor only once before the ball is released.

4

3

As you land on your left foot, bend your left knee before pushing powerfully off your left foot to perform an explosive, driving leap.

Head up, judging distance to basket

As you drive upward, your right leg bends at the knee as if you were hurdling. Stretch your body and arms up. Your focus should be on the point on the backboard that you want the ball to strike.

2

At first, you may want to push the ball up onto the backboard with your palm facing the target. As you progress and build confidence and timing with your lay-ups, try the scoop lay-up technique with your hand underneath the ball, palm facing up, so that you can send the ball up softly to the target.

Aim for the top corners of the inner rectangle marked on the backboard. Release the ball gently to bounce off the backboard and then drop down through the hoop.

PRO TIPS

Try to keep your eyes on the ball as you descend in case the shot misses and you need to leap up again for a rebound.

A reverse is a lay-up made from the opposite side of the basket. You drive under the basket and lay the ball up with your back facing the backboard. It is trickier to master but useful because the hoop helps protect your lay-up from a defensive block.

To make a regular lay-up from the right-hand side of the basket, time your movements as you take a long stride toward the basket. Stay springy on the balls of your feet.

Expect some contact when making a lay-up while under pressure from an opponent. Being determined and concentrating on your technique will give you a good chance of scoring.

Used when rebounding (see pp. 34–35) or when gathering a loose ball close to the basket, a power lay-up sees you drive powerfully up off both feet. You still need a light touch to release the ball to score.

Fouls and violations

Fouls involve illegal contact or interference with opposing players or abuse of opponents or officials. When a foul occurs, the officials on court stop the game and signal. Violations are offenses that include traveling (taking too many steps with the ball in hand), passing back into your backcourt, or double dribbling. These result in possession of the ball passing to the other team.

Heavy contact made by offensive player

Players on offense as well as defense can cause fouls. Here, a player has deliberately made heavy contact with a defender who had previously established his position. The referee will award a charging foul against the offensive player.

In your enthusiasm to pat the ball away or steal it from an opponent, you might be guilty of slapping or hitting the arms of an opponent with the ball. This is a personal foul.

Defender static but knocked back by charge

Fouls are either personal, such as tripping, or technical, such as interfering with a throw-in or fighting. If a personal foul occurs, the foul will be counted against a player, and if they receive five personal fouls (six in the NBA), they are fouled out and unable to take any further part in the game. On the court, however, their team can continue playing with five players.

Opponents must not push or grab each other

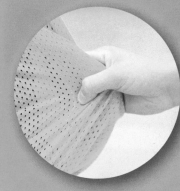

Stopping an opponent's movement by grabbing or holding a part of their body or pulling their jersey are all personal fouls.

Fouls frequently lead to free throws. These are uncontested shots taken from behind the free-throw line and are worth one point each. Any player from a team can take a free throw for a technical foul, but only the fouled player can shoot after a personal foul. A set number of offensive and defensive players stand in designated positions around the edge of the lane. If a player is fouled while shooting successfully, their team gets the shot score, plus that player is granted one free throw.

A player has up to five seconds to take each free throw. Teammates and opponents take their positions around the edge of the free-throw lane. Only in certain situations are they allowed to enter the lane to contest a rebound if the throw is not successful.

Depending on the type of foul and where it was committed, teams are awarded one, two, or even three free-throw shots.

Defenders and offensive players stand around edge of free-throw lane

Official checks that no one enters the lane before free throw is taken

Free-throw line

Shooter's feet must stay behind free-throw line

Defenders stay close to offensive players

Player with the ball

Defending

The defenders in yellow are doing an excellent close-guarding job on the offensive team. This puts the player with the ball under pressure, with no easy targets to aim a pass toward.

Defending may not be as glamorous as scoring a spectacular three-pointer, but it is crucial to your team's chances of success. Top players, such as Michael Jordan and Kevin Garnett, are fans' favorites for their spectacular offensive plays. However, they are also skilled and effective defenders who are often able to stop opponents from scoring and win back possession.

Eyes watching the player's body and the ball

Knees bent a little

The defender in blue adopts a strong defensive stance on the balls of her feet with a wide base. She is close to the offensive player but not so close that the player can just dribble past easily. Her hands are held so that they can be moved quickly to block both bounce passes and high passes.

Defending starts as soon as your team loses possession of the ball. Man-to-man guarding is the most common defensive system. It involves you guarding an opponent closely, denying them the space to receive a pass easily or threaten your basket. When guarding a player, stay light on your feet—ready to move in any direction—and keep yourself between the player and your basket.

The defender in blue tries to block an opponent's shot. Use your hand closest to the basket to make a block, as this means you do not have to reach across the opponent's body, which could result in a foul.

Try to watch the waist of the player you are guarding. While they can try to trick you with fake movements using their arms or feet, the core of their body moves only when their whole body moves. When guarding a player dribbling the ball, stay facing the player with your hands out, looking for an opportunity to flick the ball out of their control.

An alert defender in blue spots a weak, misdirected pass and pounces on it to gain possession for his team.

Masterclass

Lauren Jackson
The Seattle Storm's Lauren Jackson leaps to block a shot attempt by Diana Taurasi of the Phoenix Mercury. A tenacious defender, Jackson averages just under eight rebounds (see pp. 34–35) and two blocks per game.

When in the defensive stance, move by sliding your feet across the court floor. Firstly, move the foot closest to the direction in which you want to go.

Slide your second foot toward your first, keeping them roughly shoulder width apart. Do not cross your legs, as this can make you unbalanced.

BLOCK: when a defender manages to legally stop or deflect an attempted shot

Basketball terms

Rebounding

A large percentage of shots taken in a game are unsuccessful, even at NBA level. Many missed shots bounce back into play from either the hoop or the backboard. Rebounding is the skill of gaining possession of the ball in these situations. In a close contest, the team with the best rebounders will often win the game.

Good rebounding requires strength and determination. You can expect some contact when competing for the ball inside a crowded lane. However, rebounding also requires anticipation, timing, and great athleticism. Players must predict the bounce of the ball, get into a good position, and time their jump upward to secure the ball in both hands.

As a shot goes up, try to get into a strong rebounding position. Without fouling, get in front of your opponent and pivot around to face the basket. This is called boxing out or blocking out.

Arms out to make yourself a bigger obstacle to get around

Taking small steps to keep your opponent boxed out, look to get into the best possible position on the court floor for the rebound.

Arms extend upward quickly during jump to reach ball first

1

2

As a successful rebounder, you have to make an instant decision about your next move, as you will usually be under heavy pressure from opponents. On offense, your most likely play is to jump straight up to shoot, with a jump shot or a lay-up. If you make a defensive rebound, you may consider a drive out of your own backcourt or an outlet pass to a teammate.

This offensive player in yellow is the first to the ball. He chooses to tip it back onto the back-board, as if performing a lay-up, to try to score.

Masterclass

Dwight Howard

Dwight Howard rises high to claim another rebound for the Orlando Magic against Sacramento. A master at boxing out, Howard has led the NBA in rebounds in three seasons. In 2011, he became the first player in NBA history to be voted NBA Defensive Player of the Year for three seasons in a row.

Bend your knees and spring powerfully upward off both feet. Jump straight up, extending your arms upward and try to take the ball as early as you can, before an opponent can reach the ball.

Spread fingers around the ball to get a good grip

Securing a defensive rebound, this player makes an accurate pass over an opponent's head before that opponent can get set and block the ball. Sometimes, an outlet pass to a teammate close to the sideline will be the best play.

"Any knucklehead can score. It takes brains to rebound."

Charles Barkley, power forward and rebound master

Drill it!

To be a great basketball player, you are going to need as much training and practice as possible. In team practice sessions, you can master and perfect core skills through games and drills. Practice sessions are where you will make your greatest improvements as a player, but only if you listen to your coach and commit yourself as fully as you would in a game.

A good coach keeps practice sessions fresh by using different drills and games to test, develop, and improve players' skills. Practice sessions offer an opportunity to ask your coach any questions about the game, rules, or a particular technique. They also give you a good chance to work with other players in realistic game situations, such as rebounding or setting a screen.

This player is practicing her dribbling while weaving in and out of cones on the court floor. She aims to dribble accurately and smoothly, keeping her body balanced.

The player in yellow is practicing turning and shooting. He receives the ball with his back to the basket and an opponent close behind him.

As he pivots around smoothly, he brings the ball up into a good shooting position before taking a jump shot at the basket. The defender can attempt to block the shot.

Both players then try to get into the best position to catch the ball on the rebound should the shot miss.

These players are practicing shooting from different points. Once they have completed three successful shots in a row from one position, they will move to another.

Working on your skills should not end when team practice does. Try to get as much time with a ball as possible. Outdoor hardcourt areas will give you and friends opportunities to work on passing, receiving, dribbling, and movement. You can practice shooting on your own, while chest and bounce passes can be practiced with just a wall. Simply chalk up some target areas to aim at.

In this fast break drill, two players start in their backcourt with one passing the ball to the other.

The receiver catches the ball and dribbles up the court as fast as she can. The other player also sprints up the court.

As they get close to the basket, the free player signals for a pass. The dribbler aims her pass a little ahead for the receiver to run toward.

The receiver catches the ball in her stride as she steps into the lane and performs a lay-up to the basket. The ball is then retrieved and the drill repeated back down the court.

PRO TIPS
Training is a great opportunity to learn more about how your teammates play. Remember this information, as it can be vital in a game.

Team defense

Watch any basketball game and you'll see moments of individual defensive brilliance, such as a diving scramble for a loose ball or a spectacular shot block. Yet these individual triumphs count for nothing unless the whole team performs really well as a defensive unit throughout the whole game. Supporting your teammates and communicating well with them will help you as a team.

These are the approximate positions for defenders playing a 2–3 zone defense. The two front players—usually the shorter, quicker guards—will try to harass the other team's offense.

As a defender, you need strong individual skills, but you must also work with your teammates to keep pressure on the other team. Be aware of the game around you—you might be able to steal possession if the ball bounces loose. Also listen for calls of "switch" from a teammate who may have lost their opponent and wants you to pick them up.

An offensive player in blue is stepping in from the left to set a screen and block the defender guarding the player with the ball.

The screen is successful, and the player with the ball is free. To counter this, the defenders switch who they are guarding.

38

One defensive tactic, often used when time is running out at the end of a period, is the full-court press. This sees close man-to-man guarding right across the court, even under the defensive team's own basket.

With every defender guarding his opposing player tightly, the pressure mounts on the player with the ball, who may make a mistake. Here, the offensive player in yellow, while looking around for a safe pass, has let his dribble become loose, allowing his defender to move in and steal the ball.

Defender guarding his opponent

Some teams play different defensive systems in different game situations. Outlawed in the NBA but played in some other competitions, zone defense sees players guard an area in and around their lane and any player that enters the area. Defenders may even choose to double-team an offensive player, trying to force them into making an error.

Masterclass

Tim Duncan

Tim Duncan, playing for the San Antonio Spurs, blocks a shot by Zach Randolph of the Memphis Grizzlies. In his first ten seasons in the NBA, Duncan averaged at least two blocks and 10.6 rebounds every game. A four-time NBA champion, Duncan has been named to the NBA All Defensive Team a record 13 times.

"Talent wins games, but teamwork and intelligence win championships."

Michael Jordan, NBA legend

One-on-ones

While working with teammates will often advance your offensive play, there will be plenty of times in games when you are one-on-one with an opponent. You will want to move the ball past them, either to exploit the space behind or to make a direct drive to the basket. To do this, you can use a mixture of turns, dribbles, and fakes.

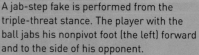

A jab-step fake is performed from the triple-threat stance. The player with the ball jabs his nonpivot foot (the left) forward and to the side of his opponent.

Strong, quick jab steps and fakes may help create an opening, but you will need good pace and dribbling skills to drive past your opponent. Always protect the ball by putting your body between it and the opponent. You can change direction and dribbling hand using a reverse or spin dribble, pivoting around so that you turn your back to your opponent before switching hands.

The player brings his left foot across his body to the right and starts a low dribble and drive past the defender, who is unbalanced as a result of the move.

The crossover dribble is a great way of changing direction suddenly, often wrong-footing the defender. Approaching an opponent, the dribbler fakes hard to her left, taking the defender in that direction.

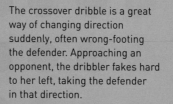

Defender's body weight shifts to her right leg

Hand kept on top of ball

The dribbler swings back, suddenly bouncing the ball low across her body from her left to her right hand.

An offensive player receives the ball with his back to the basket. He intends to perform a ball fake move.

With the ball in both hands, the player fakes a convincing turn to his left. The defender buys the fake and follows this movement.

The player pivots sharply around to his right and starts to dribble the ball past the opponent with his left hand—the hand farthest from the opponent.

You may favor one way to get past an opponent, but if you use it all the time, you will become easy to defend against. If you always try to drive past an opponent, for instance, they may back up and stand farther away from you to prevent that play. Try to mix up your fakes and moves when facing the same opponent to keep them guessing. Being able to dribble with either hand and having a full range of passes helps give you more options.

Keeping the ball on her far side away from the defender, the dribbler steps around the defender and drives away strongly. Her opponent cannot reach the ball easily, and any heavy contact is likely to result in a defensive foul.

Body between defender and ball

A defender stretches high to block a shot, but the offensive player was faking and can now reach around to make a bounce pass.

PRO TIPS
Even if you get past your defender, stay aware, as the defensive team may call a switch or you may spot a teammate in a better position than you.

Basketball terms   **SWITCH:** when defenders swap opponents they are guarding

Team offense

However much praise individual skills may get, basketball is a team game. A successful team works closely together as a unit. Players must play unselfishly, creating space and chances for teammates as well as talking to and supporting each other. Players also follow their coach's instructions on offensive plays that have been drilled in training.

Receiver's hands up and out to catch the ball

The give-and-go is one of the most common passing moves in basketball. It is a two-person play that can advance the ball up the court quickly. It starts with one player passing crisply to a teammate.

Most offensive plays have one aim—to get a player into a strong position to take a shot. If your team has a very good shooter, getting that player into position is often a priority. Don't be afraid to put your own shooting skills to the test, however, if you spot a promising opportunity.

Hand out, calling for the return pass

As soon as the pass leaves his hands, the passer sprints sharply to make a cut forward and then signals for the ball. The receiver pivots quickly to make a return pass.

On a fast break, offensive players arrange themselves into lanes. Here, two offensive players in yellow are out wide, while their three teammates play down the middle.

A fast break may be possible when a quick rebound is made or when one player forces a sudden turnover. The team now with possession must move the ball up the court as quickly as possible, but under control. The ultimate aim is to send a teammate in for a lay-up, but if that's not possible, you should quickly look for an alternative shooting option.

A coach and team huddle during a time-out. Always listen to your coach's comments and instructions during a game and share any important information about your opponents with your team.

The ball is passed back to the first player with one or more defenders cut out of the game as a result. Here, the passer has chosen to make a bounce pass aimed ahead of his teammate for him to run toward.

Masterclass

Kobe Bryant

Kobe Bryant leaps to the basket during a 2011 game between the Los Angeles Lakers and the New Orleans Hornets. Bryant is a devastating shooter, and many of his team's plays aim to get him in on the basket. He has also made more than 5,000 assists for teammates during his NBA career.

Eyes on the ball as a return pass is made

Creating space

Teammates can work together to create a useful space for a player to move into. Sometimes, a good strong cut, such as a "V" cut in and then out of the lane, will draw defenders away, creating space for others. You can also perform a screening move. Here, one player blocks the path of an opponent without committing a foul. A teammate can then dribble and drive through or move into the space created to receive a pass.

1 In this three-on-three situation, the offensive team in blue intends to make a screen away play. One player (number 21) passes the ball to a teammate on her right.

2 Having made the pass, number 21 moves forward, taking her own defender with her. She is aiming to set a screen on the defender guarding her teammate (number 20).

There are many different types of screen plays. However, they all involve one or more offensive players setting a screen by getting into position and standing still to block an opponent's path. A good screen features a wide stance so that it is harder for the defender to get around. You should also keep your arms tucked into your chest.

Speed and positioning are crucial when setting screens. You must read the play well, predict the likely moves ahead, and position yourself to block the defender's path. If you are still on the move as you make contact with the defender, there is a good chance that the officials will signal a charging foul against you. Your screen must be held until your teammate has gone by.

Setting a screen

Diante Garrett of the Iowa State Cyclones drives around a screen set by his teammate during a game against the Kansas State Wildcats. To take full advantage of a screen, the player using the screen must react smartly and move quickly around, close to their teammate.

In this simple pick-and-roll move, an offensive player in yellow spots an opportunity for his dribbling teammate to move to the left. He sets up a legal screen with a wide base and his arms folded in front of him.

The dribbler sees the screen and starts driving to his left. The opposing defender makes contact with the screen but cannot reach the dribbler as his path is blocked.

The dribbler runs close to the screen his teammate has set. Only when the dribbler has gone past does the screening player turn and move.

Offensive player moves into the open space

Number 21 sets a firm, wide base with both feet on the floor. With the defenders blocked from guarding her teammate, number 20 cuts around the screen to receive the ball.

Basketball terms **CHARGING:** a foul that occurs when a player runs into an opponent who has established their position

Great plays

"They don't pay you a million dollars for two-hand chest passes," said NBA Hall of Famer Pete Maravich. Top players love to entertain crowds with slick moves that young players can only dream of making. Many professional players are capable of incredible acts of skill and athleticism, performing unbelievable moves in the blink of an eye.

This player performs a power hook. He jumps with his front shoulder pointing to the basket while his arm that is farthest from the basket brings the ball up and over in a curving path.

1 A behind-the-back pass can switch the direction of play and sometimes catch the defense napping. The player brings the ball out wide to his right with his right hand.

2 Bringing the arm around behind his back, he drives the ball to his left with a swing of his shoulders and arm. The ball should travel directly to the receiver.

Some players become famous for certain moves, which younger players then try to copy. These signature moves range from Steve Nash's behind-the-back passes when airborne to Allen Iversen's crossover dribbles. You should enjoy trying these and other moves of the stars when you practice, but use them in a game only when you're certain, or almost certain, of success.

Masterclass

Vince Carter

Vince Carter, playing for the Orlando Magic, scores with a dunk against the Detroit Pistons. Carter is not the tallest NBA player, at 6 ft. 6 in. (1.98m), but his explosive leaping and dunking skills are well known, winning him the 2000 NBA Slam Dunk Contest.

Some moves appear fancy but, having been practiced regularly, can be used in games as high percentage plays. For example, crowds love a dunk in which the ball is driven down through the hoop, but this can often be a sensible, low-risk move when a tall forward can guide the ball down into the basket without risking a short-range shot.

This player performs a fadeaway jump shot. With an opponent close by, he angles his jump backward and stretches up with his arms to launch a shot.

Shoulders square to the basket

Both legs off the ground

Blake Griffin of the Los Angeles Clippers collects a pass thrown up to him as he flies through the air to perform a powerful dunk. This type of pass is known as an alley-oop and needs precise timing to work.

Basketball terms **HIGH PERCENTAGE:** a shot or move that has a great likelihood of success

World of basketball

Basketball is played all over the world, but different rules are used in different regions. NBA and NCAA rules are often used in the United States, while the rest of the world uses FIBA rules. Differences in these rules include various court sizes and markings. While the NBA is home to the world's strongest teams, many countries have their own leagues, and continents and regions have their own competitions.

The best players from Europe, Asia, and elsewhere may reach the NBA. Lithuania's Linas Kleiza (right) played for Olympiacos Piraeus for two seasons after a spell at the Denver Nuggets, and in 2011 he returned to the NBA to play for the Toronto Raptors.

The Euroleague, which began in 1958, is the top competition for basketball clubs in Europe. It is now a 24-team competition, with Real Madrid's eight victories making it the most successful team. Occasional games are played between the Euroleague and NBA champions. In 2010, Barcelona beat the Los Angeles Lakers 92–88.

The Atlanta Dream's Erika de Souza grabs a rebound during a WNBA game against the Seattle Storm. Founded in 1996, the 12-team WNBA is the leading league for female players and features top talent from all over the globe.

Tiago Splitter of Brazil (right) lays the ball up during the final of the 2009 FIBA Americas Championship against Puerto Rico. In a thrilling final quarter, Brazil withstood a spirited comeback by Puerto Rico to squeeze home 61–60.

Emir Preldzic passes the ball during a 2011 Euroleague game between Valencia and Preldzic's own team, Fenerbahce Ulker Istanbul.

CSKA Moscow fans celebrate as their team beats Maccabi Elite Tel Aviv 91–77 to win the 2007–2008 Euroleague title. It was the Russian team's sixth Euroleague success.

Wherever they play, professional basketball players are highly trained and focused athletes who may compete in more than 100 games a year. These games include the regular and playoff season games for their teams, participating in scrimmages and exhibition games, and representing their country in international competitions. Players need good strength and stamina to last the long season, in which bothersome injuries can occur.

Basketball terms **STAMINA:** a player's ability to perform at peak levels for long periods of time

College basketball

There is only one place in the world where the television rights for basketball played by college students costs almost $11 billion—the United States. College basketball is huge, with crowds in their thousands. The National Collegiate Athletic Association (NCAA) season reaches its climax with "March Madness," as teams compete to win the coveted NCAA Division I championships.

John Wall poses with the president and coach of the Washington Wizards in 2010. Wall joined the NBA team after just one season in college basketball for the University of Kentucky.

College basketball games are played in dozens of regional conferences around the United States. The top 31 men's conferences form the men's Division I, and the standard of basketball at this level can be exceptional. Players who thrive there often make it to the NBA. Some players play only a year of college basketball, such as Chris Bosh and John Wall, or bypass it completely, such as Kobe Bryant and LeBron James.

Matt Howard of Butler University drives past Roscoe Smith of the University of Connecticut in the NCAA Division I Men's Championship final in 2011. Howard's team lost in the low-scoring game, 41–53.

Michael Jordan helped the University of North Carolina win the NCAA championship in 1982. He averaged 17.7 points and 1.8 assists per game in the 101 games that he played before entering the NBA.

> *"If you have talent with teamwork, you've got a chance to be a championship team."*
>
> *Mike Krzyzewski,*
> *Duke University coach*

College basketball legend Herb Magee has coached at Philadelphia University for more than 45 years. He has won more than 900 college games as coach.

Women's college basketball is organized along similar lines to the men's game, with 64 teams competing to win the prestigious Division I Women's Championship. The University of Tennessee is the most successful women's team, with eight titles, although the University of Connecticut are right behind, with seven championships.

Sydney Colson of Texas A&M University looks for a way past the University of Notre Dame's Frederica Miller in the final of the 2010–2011 NCAA Division I Women's Championship. The Aggies won 76–70, securing their first ever national championship.

Basketball terms **ASSIST:** a pass to a teammate that directly leads to scoring a basket

Legendary center Wilt Chamberlain makes one of the 23,924 rebounds of his NBA career. Here, he is playing against the Milwaukee Bucks in 1972, the year he won the NBA championship for the second time.

The NBA

The National Basketball Association (NBA) was formed in 1949 from the merger of two professional leagues, the BBA and the NBL. It has grown into 30 teams split into Western and Eastern conferences, each with three divisions of five teams. The NBA eclipses all other basketball leagues around the world both in popularity and in quality, and the cream of the world's talent flocks to play in it.

Drama and controversy, fierce passion, and extraordinary action are all part of a typical NBA season. The games come thick and fast, with the very best players influencing results game after game. These players are the sport's superstars, becoming major celebrities who are rewarded with large salaries and sponsorship deals.

Australian Andrew Bogut dribbles the ball for the Milwaukee Bucks. Bogut is one of more than 80 foreign players on the rosters of NBA teams. These foreign players come from countries as far afield as China, Argentina, Tanzania, and Russia.

> ## "Coaching in the NBA is not easy. It's like a nervous breakdown with a paycheck."
>
> *Pat Williams, Orlando Magic cofounder*

The two conferences clash at All-Star Weekend in February, with an East versus West game featuring players picked by fan vote. Here, the West's Kobe Bryant keeps possession away from the East's Ray Allan. Bryant was the top scorer in six of the seven 2010 NBA Finals games and has won five NBA championships.

Players, fans, and coaches all feel the strain of an NBA season, which starts competitively at the end of October. Teams play 82 regular season games, 41 at home in large arenas mostly packed with home fans, and 41 on the road. The eight best teams in each conference enter the playoffs in April. The aim is to win their way through three best-of-seven-game knockout rounds to play in the championship finals, which is another best-of-seven series.

Phoenix Suns fans, dressed in their orange outfits, cheer on their team during the 2010 NBA Playoffs at the US Airways Center in Arizona. NBA rivalries arouse strong passions among loyal fans.

The Boston Celtics' Kevin Garnet (right) leaps to the basket during the last game of the 2010 NBA Finals against the Los Angeles Lakers. These Celtics and the Lakers are the most successful teams in the NBA. The Celtics have won 17 championships, while the Lakers, who triumphed 4–3 in this series, have won 16.

ROSTER: the list of players on a basketball team

Basketball terms

International games

The pinnacles of international basketball are the summer Olympic Games and the basketball World Cup. Only a handful of the very best national teams manage to qualify for either tournament. They are both played in a pool format followed by a knockout round leading to a single-game final.

Members of the Soviet Union team hug after recording the U.S.A.'s first ever Olympic defeat in 1972. The U.S.A. team refused to collect their silver medals in protest, and they still remain at the International Olympic Committee's headquarters in Switzerland.

Teams from the Philippines and Mexico compete in the 1936 Olympics. The tournament was played on outside courts that turned to mud in the rain. The U.S.A. beat Canada 19–8 in the low-scoring final.

Superstars from the original U.S.A. Dream Team for the 1992 Olympics: (left–right) Michael Jordan, Patrick Ewing, Magic Johnson, Karl Malone, and Charles Barkley.

The U.S.A. has dominated Olympic basketball, with the men going unbeaten in Olympic competition before suffering a controversial gold-medal match defeat at the hands of the Soviet Union in 1972. Four years later, women's basketball debuted at the Olympics, and the U.S.A has dominated the competition. Professional players were allowed to compete from 1992 onward, but shocks have still continued, such as Argentina's 89–81 defeat of the U.S.A. men's team in 2004.

Australia's Tully Bevilaqua drives to the basket against Kara Lawson of the U.S.A. team during the final of the women's 2008 Olympic competition. Australia won silver at three consecutive Olympics from 2000.

Spain's Rudy Fernandez dribbles the ball during the final of the 2008 men's Olympic competition in Beijing, China. Spain beat Greece, China, Croatia, and Lithuania on its way to the final.

The U.S.A. men's basketball team, captained by Kobe Bryant, wave on the medal podium ready to receive their 2008 Olympic gold medals after pulling away from Spain in the fourth quarter to win 117–108.

The FIBA world championship was first held in 1950 and is now known as the World Cup, featuring 24 teams in both the men's and women's competitions. The former republic of Yugoslavia has won the men's competition five times, while Spain won in 2006 and the U.S.A. in 2010. The women's tournament began in 1953. While the U.S.A. has dominated the competition, 17 different nations, including Cuba, Japan, Brazil, and Australia, have won medals.

Michaela Ferancikova of the Czech Republic looks to block Diana Taurasi during the 2010 world championship final. The game ended in a U.S.A. victory, 89–69, the eighth time the U.S.A. women's team has been crowned world champions.

Hidayet Türkoglu of Turkey looks to drive past members of the Ivory Coast team during the 2010 FIBA World Championships. Turkey beat France, Slovenia, and Serbia in the knockout stages before falling to the U.S. team in the final, 81–64.

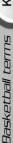

Basketball legends

Since its invention, the great game of basketball has been graced by hundreds of outstanding male and female players. Some showed great athleticism and explosive skills, while others exhibited steely determination, great vision, and tactical awareness.

Manu Ginobili

Ginobili was a Euroleague winner with Kinder Bologna and 2004 Olympic gold medalist with Argentina. This powerful shooting guard completed the full set of top-flight honors with the San Antonio Spurs, winning three NBA championships.

Wilt Chamberlain

Wilt "the Stilt" was no ordinary center. Standing 7 ft. 1 in. (2.16m) tall, he towered over many players during the 1960s. He had excellent skills and averaged 30.1 points per game during his 1,045 games. He was a superb rebounder, leading the NBA in rebounds in 11 seasons and making 23,924 rebounds throughout his NBA career.

Larry Bird

In the 1978 draft, the Boston Celtics picked up an Indiana State forward who became one of the greatest ever all-around players. Bird (right) was adept at all parts of the game, notching, on average, more than 24 points, 10 rebounds, and 6 assists per NBA game. He won three NBA championships with the Celtics.

Oscar Schmidt

Brazil's greatest ever player, Schmidt played at five Olympic Games in the 1980s and 1990s and was the top scorer at three of them, but he always resisted overtures from NBA teams to turn professional. Even so, he scored a record 49,703 points in top-level competition in Italy, Spain, and Brazil.

Lisa Leslie

A four-time Olympic gold medalist and stalwart of the Los Angeles Spark WNBA team, Leslie usually played center. In 2002, she became the first woman to perform a slam dunk in the WNBA.

Julius Erving

Only one NBA championship ever came Dr. J's way in 1983 with the Philadelphia 76ers, but his status in the game is assured with some of the most spectacular plays ever seen in professional basketball. Playing for the Virginia Squires and New York Nets in the ABA before joining the 76ers in 1976, Erving (left) popularised massive slam dunks and innovative offensive moves to the basket, scoring 30,026 NBA points in the process.

Kobe Bryant

Drafted by the Charlotte Hornets in 1996 when he was just 17, Bryant was traded to the Los Angeles Lakers, with whom he has won five NBA championships. Bryant's ability to get off an accurate shot from almost anywhere on the court is legendary. His 81 points in a single game against the Toronto Raptors in 2006 is a record for a 21st-century NBA player.

Basketball terms **DRAFT**: a way that teams choose players to enter professional basketball

Irwin "Magic" Johnson

The architect of the Los Angeles Lakers' fast-moving "Showtime" offense during the 1980s, Johnson (center) was one of the most creative players to grace basketball. Over more than 900 NBA games, Johnson averaged 11.2 assists per game—an NBA record. Backed by a strong all-around game, which included 17,707 total points scored and an average of 7.72 rebounds per game, Johnson helped the Lakers to six NBA championships.

Kareem Abdul-Jabbar

When he retired in 1989 after 20 seasons in the NBA with the Milwaukee Bucks and Los Angeles Lakers, this center held almost every NBA record worth having. He is still the NBA's leading points scorer, with 38,387, and holds the record for the most field goals, with 15,387.

Michael Jordan

The most famous, marketed, and possibly greatest basketball player of all time, Jordan (number 23) entered the NBA in 1984. He helped the Chicago Bulls to six NBA championships, led the NBA points scoring tables for ten different seasons, and won two Olympic gold medals. Renowned for his hang time, Jordan scored 32,292 points in the NBA and notched 2,514 steals. Yet for all his offensive prowess, Jordan was also a superb defender able to harass, block, and rebound seemingly at will.

Lauren Jackson

A formidable opponent on offense and defense, this Australian has played for the Seattle Storm in the WNBA since 2001. Internationally, she has been part of an Australian team that has earned three Olympic silver medals and won the 2006 FIBA World Championship.

Cheryl Miller

Miller drove teams to success throughout her career. She led her high school team to 132 wins out of 136 games from 1978–1982, and placed fifth among the NCAA's all-time points scorers and third on its most successful rebounders table while playing for the University of Southern California.

Dirk Nowitzki

After more than a decade with the Dallas Mavericks, Nowitzki helped his team win the 2011 NBA championship and became the first European to be voted the NBA's Most Valuable Player.

LeBron James

After being drafted by the Cleveland Cavaliers in 2003, James began his NBA career with an impressive 25 points, nine assists, six rebounds, and four steals in his first game. A powerful presence all over the court, he won Rookie of the Year in his first season. In 2010, James became a free agent and a TV special was broadcast nationally in which he announced that he would sign for the Miami Heat.

Yao Ming

At 7 ft. 6 in. (2.29m), Ming is one of the NBA's tallest players. He played for the Shanghai Sharks before joining the Houston Rockets in 2002 and has made an impact on and off the court. He was an NBA All-Star Game pick eight times.

Basketball terms **FREE AGENT**: a player able to sign a contract to play with any team

Showtime!

A fiercely contested major basketball game is usually great entertainment in itself. However, some players and teams like to give fans a little bit extra. This includes entertainment before and during games, three-point and half-court shooting contests, and jam sessions where fans get the chance to meet players. In addition, there are fun variations of the sport to watch or try.

During a halftime show, Detroit Shock's mascot Zap gets enormous air off a small trampoline to perform an outrageous flying dunk.

22 | HORNBUCKLE'S BALLERS

All-Star Weekend in February is many fans' favorite part of the NBA season. It's a time of fun, action, and competitions, including flying leaps and plenty of slam dunk events. At its center is the All Star Game, pitting players selected by fan vote from Eastern Conference and Western Conference teams. The game's emphasis is on fancy plays and all-out offense and is usually high scoring—in 2011, the West beat the East 148–143.

A Harlem Globetrotter hangs from the basket during a game in Spain. The team pioneered basketball entertainment with outrageous moves. The Globetrotters' legendary Curly Neal, for example, could kick the ball to score a basket from the midcourt line.

A mascot for the Atlanta Hawks rides a unicycle around the court. Mascots are a feature of NBA and college basketball, whipping up the crowd and becoming a part of the entertainment.

The glass backboard shatters as Darryl Dawkins launches an enormous slam dunk while playing for the Philadelphia 76ers against the Kansas City Kings in 1979. The much-traveled Dawkins repeated the feat three weeks later, resulting in the NBA making it a suspension offense.

You'll find basketball played in some strange places and in unusual ways if you look hard enough. One such example is unicycle basketball, which uses a regular ball and court but with all of the players riding unicycles. This crazy sport even has its North American championships, with leading teams including the Berkeley Revolution and the Puerto Rico All Stars.

Children and teens in Havana, Cuba, play a game of street ball. With less emphasis on rules and more emphasis on individual play, street ball games sometimes shrink to two-on-two played on half a court.

"When I dunk, I put something on it. I want the ball to hit the floor before I do."

Darryl Dawkins, slam dunk maestro

Glossary

assist
A pass to a teammate that directly leads to scoring a basket.

backboard
The rectangular or fan-shaped board that the hoop is attached to.

backcourt
The half of the court that a team is defending.

block
A blocked shot, when defenders deflect or stop a shot attempt with their hand while the ball is still on its upward flight.

bounce pass
A pass in which the ball is bounced on the floor before it reaches the receiver.

boxing out
A technique during rebounding in which one player gets their body in front of the basket and also in front of their opponent to obtain a better position to collect the rebound.

center
A player position usually taken by the tallest player on the team.

charging
A foul that occurs when a player runs into an opponent who has established their position.

cut
A sharp run made by an offensive player without the ball to find space.

double dribble
A violation that occurs when a player dribbles the ball, catches it, then dribbles again, or dribbles with both hands at the same time.

double team
When two teammates guard a single opponent between them.

draft
The way teams choose players who are moving from college or sometimes high school basketball to professional basketball.

drive
A fast, aggressive dribble and move toward the basket.

dunk
When a player jumps and throws or forces the ball down into the basket.

end line
The boundary line at each end of the court; also called the baseline.

fake
A move made to deceive a defender to throw them off balance and allow the offensive player to receive a pass or make a pass or shot themselves.

fast break
A play in which offensive players take the ball and move it quickly from their backcourt to their frontcourt before the defensive team can regroup.

feint
See "fake."

FIBA
The shortened name of the International Basketball Federation, the organization that runs basketball in much of the world.

forward
A player who tends to play close to the basket and is a good close-range shooter and rebounder.

free agent
In many professional leagues, this describes a player able to sign a contract to play with any team.

free throw
An opportunity to score one point, free of defenders, from the free-throw line in front of the basket.

free-throw lane
Also known as the paint, this is the rectangular area marked by lines underneath each basket.

frontcourt
The half of the court where a team on offensive can score.

guards
Positions usually taken by players who are excellent offensive players and good at long-range shooting.

hang time
The amount of time a player can stay in the air when shooting the ball.

hook shot
A one-handed overhead shot with the arm looking like a hook.

knockout
A type of competition in which the winning team in a game progresses to the next round while the losing team goes out of the competition.

MVP
Short for most valuable player, an award made to the most outstanding player in a game, series, or season.

offensive foul
When an offensive player makes illegal contact with an opponent.

open
A term used to describe a player on the offensive team who is in a position to receive a pass.

outlet pass
A pass made by a defensive rebounder to a teammate who has more space and is under less pressure.

overtime
An extra period of playing time added at the end of normal time if the score is tied.

Paralympic Games
A multisport event held shortly after the Olympics for elite athletes with disabilities.

personal foul
A player foul which involves illegal contact with an opposing player.

pivoting
The act of keeping one foot in place but swiveling and stepping around with the other foot.

rebound
When an unsuccessful shot bounces off the rim or the backboard and one player gathers the ball.

screen
An offensive play used to block an opponent from reaching another part of the court.

shot clock
The clock that displays the time a team with the ball has left to shoot.

stamina
A player's ability to perform at peak levels for long periods of time.

steal
To gain possession of the ball from an opponent.

switch
When defenders change the person they are guarding.

time-out
A break in play, usually one minute long, requested by a team.

tip-off
A way of starting a basketball game in which the referee throws the ball up in the air and opposing players try to pat the ball to a teammate.

traveling
A violation in which you take too many steps after catching the ball.

triple-threat stance
A stance taken by a player with the ball, from which they can potentially either dribble, pass, or shoot.

turnover
When an offensive team loses possession without scoring.

violation
A breaking of the rules of the game, such as a double dribble.

Websites

www.nba.com
The official website of the National Basketball Association (NBA) is packed with features, statistics on players and teams, and links to the Women's NBA.

www.fiba.com
The official website of the International Basketball Federation (FIBA) includes simple and full rules of the sport, plus coaching tips, results, and player interviews.

www.helpfulhoops.com
A collection of more than 1,100 drills and exercises to improve every aspect of your basketball game, from warming up to shooting, passing, and game tactics.

www.ihoops.com
An online community for youth basketball, this website includes tips, drills, player position guides, and much more.

www.basketball-reference.com
A phenomenal stats and records website containing details of every NBA season, plus All-Star Games and other competitions.

www.hoophall.com
This website contains details of the hundreds of players and coaches who have been honored in the Naismith Memorial Basketball Hall of Fame.

www.eurobasket.com
Despite its European title, this comprehensive website carries news and results from major basketball competitions all over the world.

Index

Picture credits

The publisher would like to thank the following for permission to reproduce their material. Every care has been taken to trace copyright holders. However, if there have been unintentional omissions or failure to trace copyright holders, we apologize and will, if informed, endeavor to make corrections in any future edition.

t = top; b = bottom; c = center; l = left; r = right

Cover: Shutterstock/Elena Yakusheva, Martin Allinger and Volha Hubskaya. 6bl © Bettmann/CORBIS, 6–7 NBAE/Getty Images, 7tr Getty Images, 7cr Getty Images, 7br Time & Life Pictures/Getty Images, 9tr MCT via Getty Images, 15bl NBAE/Getty Images, 15bl NBAE/Getty Images, 23tl NBAE/Getty Images, 25br NBAE/Getty Images, 27tl Getty Images, 33bl NBAE/Getty Images, 35tl NBAE/Getty Images, 39br Getty Images, 43tl NBAE/Getty Images, 43tr NBAE/Getty Images, 45tl Getty Images, 47bl NBAE/Getty Images, 47tl NBAE/Getty Images, 48bl EB via Getty Images, 48br NBAE/Getty Images, 49r EB via Getty Images, 49br Getty Images, 48–49t AFP/Getty Images, 50bl Sports Illustrated/Getty Images, 50lc NBAE/Getty Images, 51c Sports Illustrated/Getty Images, 51tr NBAE/Getty Images, p51br Getty Images, 52l Sports Illustrated/Getty Images, p52bc NBAE/Getty Images, 53bc NBAE/Getty Images, 53tr AFP/Getty Images, 53br NBAE/Getty Images, 54cl Time & Life Pictures/Getty Images, 54bl Sports Illustrated/Getty Images, 54c Popperfoto/Getty Images, 55c Getty Images, 55tl NBAE/Getty Images, 55tc Sports Illustrated/Getty Images, p55tr Bloomberg via Getty Images, p55br AFP/Getty Images, 56l Getty Images, 56–57c NBAE/Getty Images, 57tr NBAE/Getty Images, 57br NBAE/Getty Images, 58l NBAE/Getty Images, 58c Sports Illustrated/Getty Images, 59tc NBAE/Getty Images, 59cm NBAE/Getty Images, 59cbl NBAE/Getty Images, 59cr NBAE/Getty Images, 60c NBAE/Getty Images, 60bc AFP/Getty Images, 61tl NBAE/Getty Images, 61tr © Bettmann/Corbis, 61br Sports Illustrated/Getty Images